JOHANN SEBASTIAN BACH

JESU, JOY OF MAN'S DESIRING
JESU BLEIBET MEINE FREUDE

For Violin and Piano / Für Violine und Klavier

from / aus
Cantata BWV 147

Arranged by / Bearbeitet von
Arthur Campbell

EIGENTUM DES VERLEGERS · ALLE RECHTE VORBEHALTEN
ALL RIGHTS RESERVED

EDITION PETERS
London · Frankfurt/M. · Leipzig · New York

Jesu, Joy of Man's Desiring
Jesu bleibet meine Freude

J. S. Bach
arr. Arthur Campbell

Edition Peters No. 7360
© Copyright 1992 by Hinrichsen Edition, Peters Edition Ltd., London

JOHANN SEBASTIAN BACH

JESU, JOY OF MAN'S DESIRING
JESU BLEIBET MEINE FREUDE

For Violin and Piano / Für Violine und Klavier

from / aus
Cantata BWV 147

Arranged by / Bearbeitet von
Arthur Campbell

Violin / Violine

EIGENTUM DES VERLEGERS · ALLE RECHTE VORBEHALTEN
ALL RIGHTS RESERVED

EDITION PETERS
London · Frankfurt/M. · Leipzig · New York

Jesu, Joy of Man's Desiring
Jesu bleibet meine Freude